TIME FOR KIDS READERS

OLD NEW AMSTERDAM

by Randi Hacker

Orlando   Austin   Chicago   New York   Toronto   London   San Diego

Visit *The Learning Site!*
www.harcourtschool.com

New York City is known today as a great modern city that is home to almost eight million people from all over the world. You may be surprised to know that the island of Manhattan was once a Dutch village with pigs and chickens running through the streets. This is the story of how Manhattan and the now famous New York City began during colonial times.

The first explorer to come to what is known today as New York was an Italian named Giovanni da Verrazano. He claimed the island and all the areas surrounding it for the King of France, Francis I. Unfortunately for Verrazano and for France, the discovery was not recognized or appreciated, because France was busy fighting a war with Spain. Today the only sign that Verrazano ever landed in New York is a bridge that is named after him.

Henry Hudson

It was not until 85 years later that Europeans reappeared in the area. When the Dutch arrived, the Mannahata and other Native American tribes were living there. The Dutch expedition was led by an Englishman named Henry Hudson. He was searching for a secret passage to China and Japan. He hoped it would be shorter than the route around the southern tip of South America. Hudson's discovery of the island of Manhattan was an accident. On September 3, 1609, he entered the Bay of New York thinking that it would take him to China or at least to the Pacific Ocean. Although Hudson did not find the passage, he did claim the land for the Dutch. He opened the route for others to follow.

In 1609 Henry Hudson sailed the *Half Moon* up a river that was later named the *Hudson* in his honor.

For the next 11 years Dutch settlers established trading posts along the shores of the Hudson River, named for Henry Hudson. At first the colony was called New Netherland. The area included parts of what are now Delaware, Pennsylvania, New York, New Jersey, Long Island, and Connecticut. Sailing ships carrying goods such as furs regularly sailed back and forth between Amsterdam in the Netherlands and New Netherland. As the fur trade grew so did the need for Dutch control over the settlers and the trading that was going on.

Peter Minuit

In 1621, the Dutch West India Company was formed. Not only could it set up colonies for the Old World, it could set rules for them, too. The company acted as the government for the new colony. One of its main goals was to get settlers to go there. The Dutch West India Company was the first to encourage immigrants from other countries to go to their colony in the New World. They appointed a man named Peter Minuit to be leader.

Peter Minuit built a fort at the southern tip of Manhattan Island. He called it Fort Amsterdam after the capital city of the Netherlands. Minuit helped the settlers start farms. Farming and trading furs became the way settlers survived. In time, the settlers learned to drain and fill swampy areas to create land on which they could build. The settlement at the tip of Manhattan Island was renamed New Amsterdam. It became a bustling port city where a shipbuilding industry was formed.

During Minuit's time in New Amsterdam, he worked with the Native Americans who were there when the Dutch arrived. The Lenape tribe had three main groups. Each spoke a different dialect of the Algonkin (al•GAHN•kuhn) language. These peaceful hunter-gatherers taught the settlers how to farm.

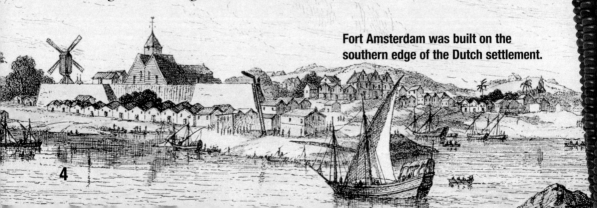

Fort Amsterdam was built on the southern edge of the Dutch settlement.

Lenape Indians lived in long houses. They grew corn, squash and beans, which were often called "the three sisters."

This painting shows what the sale of Manhattan Island might have looked like when it was bought by Peter Minuit in 1626.

In 1626 Minuit may have done what no other European explorer and settler had ever done. He made a deal with the Lenape to buy Manhattan from them. He arranged to pay for the island of Manhattan with goods, such as cloth and kettles, beads, ribbons, and other shiny trinkets.

The Lenape were probably surprised by Minuit's offer to buy the land. Native American legends claim that the Lenape chief went back to his people laughing. When asked what was so funny, he replied, "The joke is on the white men. Everyone knows you can't own land."

But own land they did. Other Dutch settlements began to spring up and grow. One of the earliest was Fort Orange, where Albany, New York, stands today. The Dutch also built Fort Good Hope, which later became Hartford, Connecticut, on the banks of the Connecticut River.

No paper record of the sale of Manhattan Island exists, but a record of a similar deal by Minuit does. He bought what is now Staten Island, across New York harbor. The bill of sale for that deal shows that Peter Minuit and five other colonists bought the island for "duffel cloth, kettles, axes, hoes, wampum, drilling awls, 'Jew's Harps'—[a kind of musical instrument]—and diverse other wares." Today, Staten Island, like Manhattan, is a borough of New York City. A borough is an area of a city.

Once the Dutch West India Company owned the island, more colonists started to arrive. Colonists established their own schools and set up their own churches. And, to get more land, they attacked the Indians in the area to force them out.

By 1650, the settlement of New Amsterdam had about 1,000 people. Houses stood along narrow dirt lanes. Pigs and chickens ran loose through the streets. Farms dotted the area around the main town.

New Amsterdam has been described as "a miniature replica of a typical Dutch city." Most Dutch houses were $1\frac{1}{2}$ stories tall. They usually had doors with two parts: a top and a bottom. People would leave the bottom half closed and open the top half to let in some fresh air. Today these doors are still called Dutch doors.

The Dutch people dressed practically. In the 1600s, men wore wigs and women wore linen caps to cover their long hair. Babies and toddlers wore long dresses, whether they were girls or boys.

The windows and roofs of houses in New Amsterdam made it look like a Dutch city.

On a typical day, people went about their work, including farming and shipbuilding.

Dutch children played some games that children today might play: marbles, hopscotch, and leapfrog. The children liked to fly kites, too. Mothers taught their daughters to raise food in a garden, to sew, and to cook. Fathers taught their sons to farm, hunt, and build. Some children attended school. Some schools were called free schools. The word *free* didn't mean that they didn't cost anything. Parents had to pay for their children to study there. The word *free* meant they weren't religious schools. They were free of the church.

Though most of the settlers were Dutch, there were people from many countries to be found in Manhattan. Sailors and traders from different European nations stopped there. African servants and sailors could be seen in the town. In 1643, a Roman Catholic missionary walked down one of the dirt streets of the town. He is said to have heard 18 different languages being spoken!

Back in the Netherlands, the Dutch West India Company grew unhappy with Minuit. The authorities felt he had made poor economic choices. Beginning in 1632, a series of men were assigned to replace Minuit. Each was dismissed for one reason or another.

Peter Stuyvesant surrendered New Amsterdam to the British on September 8, 1664.

Then in 1647 came Peter Stuyvesant, the last Dutch director general of New Netherland. Before coming to North America he had been the governor of Curacao, a Dutch colony in the Caribbean. Stuyvesant was a harsh ruler. He liked his word to be law. He allowed no religious freedom and made life very difficult for religious groups other than his own. He particularly disliked the Quakers. That kept the numbers of colonists down, which didn't please Stuyvesant's bosses. They overruled him and allowed some Protestants and Jews to join the colony. Between 1653 and 1664, New Amsterdam grew rapidly.

The British and the Dutch ended up fighting many battles over the ownership of New Amsterdam. Naval wars were fought for 22 years. The Dutch managed to hold on. Then in 1664, English warships sailed into New York harbor. On September 8, they forced Governor Peter Stuyvesant to surrender. The British changed the name of the colony to New York to honor the Duke of York. They replaced Stuyvesant with a governor of their own, Richard Nicholls. On November 10, 1664, a new era began for New York.

Though he was no longer in charge, Stuyvesant spent the rest of his life on his large farm in Manhattan. He is buried beneath what was once his chapel and is now St. Mark's Church in the Bowery, a street and section in Lower Manhattan.

THE DUTCH WEST INDIA COMPANY

The Netherlands, formerly called Holland, was a country with big plans in the 1600s. The Dutch sent ships all over the world to start colonies and to trade goods. The Dutch East India Company was in charge of Holland's colonies in Asia, including Indonesia, China, and Hong Kong. The Dutch West India Company controlled trade in the Americas.

The Dutch West India Company was a monopoly, meaning it had total control and no competition. When Holland was a strong power, no one could trade anywhere in the New World without permission from the Dutch West India Company. It controlled all the trade with West Africa, too.

The Dutch West India Company built and ruled Fort Orange, Fort Good Hope, and Fort Amsterdam. The company remained very powerful for many years. Then it began to lose money. By 1791, the Dutch West India Company was out of business.

New York grew quickly under the English. By 1700, just 36 years after the end of Dutch rule, there were more than 3 times as many people in New York. By this time, buildings filled lower Manhattan. The first newspaper, *The New-York Gazette*, was started in 1725. English replaced Dutch as the main language. The Anglican Church replaced the Dutch Reformed Church as the government's church of choice.

The Dutch colonists left their mark, though. The name of the Catskill Mountains came from the Dutch. Other places and towns have Dutch names that end in *kill*, which means "creek," like Peekskill, New York. The Bouwerie, a street in lower Manhattan now spelled Bowery, is also from a Dutch word. The character Rip van Winkle in *The Legend of Sleepy Hollow* is a descendant of Dutch settlers.

The publisher of *The New-York Gazette* didn't waste space on illustrations!

In the Catskill Mountains, places such as Plattekill still have Dutch names.

By the late 1700s, buildings in New York looked a lot like those in London, England.

Much about Manhattan has changed in the 350 years since the Dutch first arrived. But some details remain the same. New York is still a home and a meeting place for people from all over the world. The priest who heard 18 languages being spoken in New York in 1641 would hear hundreds spoken there today.

New York has grown into one of the greatest cities in the world.

Only a few of the buildings of New Amsterdam still stand—a home here, a church there. Yet some of the oldest houses in New York City are narrow and long from front to back because they were built in the Dutch style. Some of the streets of New York follow the paths first made by the Dutch. A person standing on Wall Street today, among the towering sky-scrapers, might be standing just where Peter Minuit once stood.

- Today there is a street called the Bowery in lower Manhattan. The word "*bouwerie*" (BOW•uh•ree) means "farm" in Dutch.

- The population of Manhattan today is almost 2,000 times greater than the population of New Amsterdam in 1653.

- There's another New Amsterdam. It's in Guyana, in South America.

The Bowery, 1831

The Bowery, 1976

The Bowery, 1895